American

Anywhere is the center of the world.
—*Black Elk*

. . . the faith that came out of the ground.
—*Sherwood Anderson*

AMERIC★N HANDBOOK

David Steingass

University of Pittsburgh Press

Special thanks to Nancy McCloskey for technical assistance; to Bob and Mary Ross, the MacDowell Colony, and The Ringer Family Commune for the provision of New Hampshire and California studios; and to the University of Wisconsin at Stevens Point for a leave during which much of this book was written.

Some of the poems in this volume first appeared in the following publications: *The Abraxas/5 Anthology, Choice, December, The Dragonfly, Edge* (New Zealand), *Hawaii Literary Review, Hearse, Madrona, Maine Times, New Letters, The North American Review, Northeast, Northwest Review, The Ohio Review, Pebble, Poetry Northwest, Sticks and Stones Anthology, Three Rivers Poetry Journal, Tri-Quarterly,* and *The Windsor Review.*

Library of Congress Cataloging in Publication Data

Steingass, David.
    American handbook.

    (Pitt poetry series)
    I. Title.
    PS3569.T378A8   811'.5'4   73–5370
    ISBN 0–8229–3270–9
    ISBN 0–8229–5239–4 (pbk.)

For Susan Sorrento

CONTENTS

I

This Hard Honor

Growing Into Day

Ground squirrels
Tick through dry leaves like grass fires.
The porch daydreams, shuffling mossy feet.
My sleeping dog groans.
Spruce and birch limbs slowly saw
Each other's scars. The harbor bell buoy's
Laconic, squeeze-toy tolling
Takes over the day. I feel my breath drift out with it, and
Catching the bell miss a wave
Ebb and doze into marrow-deep indolence . . .
The way blood from a cut finger
Threads the eye of a stream.

Too far up, a plane
Flickers like sunspots. Its drone
Mingles with the far waves in seashells,
A dream of hollow sound:
Rocks float through dark water, clunk
Against each other.

Suddenly I am exhausted, numb
As pigs' knuckles. Only my eyes slide.
Water bead on a red oak's palm,
I hold on, listening to the dog's white-eyed freeze
Ear-pricked, tremulous seconds.
I become what she listens for, and watch
For motion and effect:
The quiver of birds, rippling
Grass tips, the dying of sound in the air
And its fall.

Autumns of damp leaves settle,
Root the cliff dwelling, natural Gothic
Of our lives.

This Hard Honor

I look east over New England
From this barn of a covered bridge.
Dense asterisks of rolling hills,
Bright white villages
The forest gradually returns to.
Granite boundries
Rise like petrified plant sets:
One huge garden
Stretched through morning sun to the sea.
Rows of maple syrup, cider lakes,
The Acadian hills at last,
Flanked by parsley snippet islands.

Snow has colonized everything but this
Smooth wooden locomotive
Of an island. The bridge is closed,
Its road a cow's path.
Fields wait to cross, like old friends
Stand in line. A fox has left
His lope and tail plop on the river.
I close my eyes:
A Chinese-bandit raccoon
Loafs and chitters, dragging a burlap sack
Full of Rhode Island Reds
Through the powder snow.

The best part:
Standing in the middle of the road
Hanging over the Connecticut,
Halfway between New England
                              and the rest.

October Haiku

The last white birch leaves
dawn's unending plunge, deep blue
crystalline applause

Ben Franklin's Plain Song

I am the odor of hickory nuts
In autumn afternoons, galvanized
Against flame and contentment.
I burn in the soil like quicklime seeds.
I wait with the calmness of color,
Assessing you from pumpkins:
Old man ajar with himself.

Scything the Lawn by the Ocean

I lock each elbow and swing the blade
Horizontal as the sea. Tendrils
Knot over my feet, mosquitoes
Big as ichneumon flies
Flutter from harbor.
           The way my dog
Bellies through dagger ferns, nipping thistles.
Half-sunk in some pond, a moose calf grazes,
Sawing a cud of bees trapped in lilies.
Scabrous roots and shale splinters
Wash into sight
Under my blade. The way earth lies beached,
Etching through its hide.

The lawn is a felt swirl of high tide
Diaphanous in afternoon sun.
The unutterable sweetness of bled grasses.
I strain for each odor . . . the pleasure
Of old friends' speech.
             The dog rolls joyously,
Paws raking air, legs mottled squaw trees,
Back and fur one mindless jigger: spring
Colt, calf whale, dolphin
Of joy.

Backed against this spruce, I see the world
Fall away in sweet stubble.
How recently a sea of fishes
Mowed this land dry
With double-edged death and odor!
I feel numb and vague,
Half-drowned in my destruction.

Wedging

Stand a trunk section on end.
Choose the longest hairline crack
   through the closed gates of earth.

Gripping the throat of the sledge, tap
The smallest wedge, ping, ping, into the tree:
   steel woodpeckers spring to life.

Swell the split, the large wedge
Relieving its companion
   down the journey to the heartland.

Swing full strokes on each wedge.
Feel the ground at the end of your arc:
   blood churns in underground streams.

Hardwood comes best, except elm: ash
And oak, rock maple, white birch
   fall open into glowing apple halves.

The marbled quality of maple
Gives up hard, sending some of itself back
Through the sledge handle:
   stone giants guarding bone.

Piles of white marble.
Fillets of persistence
   gleaming for my exhaustion.

stone giants guarding bone
fall open into glowing apple halves.
blood churns in underground streams
down the journey to the heartland.
steel woodpeckers spring to life
through the closed gates of earth
gleaming for my exhaustion.

Three Houses

On the Jonesport Road
No one I knew could say whose.
Empty, it stood numb and swaybacked
Through Maine winters, stunned:
Its kitchen, garage, woodshed and barn
The sluggish vein
To a root cellar chiseled in bedrock
By the sea's head tide.

Began to corkscrew, slowly
Pulling something of itself
Back into the cellar.
Clapboards warped like ship's siding.
Flooring pitched, hallways buckled,
The fireplace sprawled. At night
Phosphorescent corners: doors
To the other side of the world.
The moon escaped from the chimney
As though the house popped her lid.

The *Jonesport House*
Slipped late from harbor, bound
For her lost days.
                    And collapsed.

In Haverhill, N.H.

for Bob and Mary Ross

Stood before pine and locust
Volunteered support at every wing.
Staring from the high ceilings of their lives,
Former owners hang glassy-eyed:
Backwater uncles, isolated in Russian novels.
The rooms nest, distinct as so many
One-act plays. The Connecticut River's valley
Through the windows, winds primitive and dry
Over three study walls of mural.
A twin-spired Tudor mansion on the fourth wall:
Its banner blows east, its smoke west.
Green shutters swing away in my hands
Cobwebs for nails!
The chimney's mortar shows open spaces.
I imagine the thin bricks hanging
In air, an X ray of this site. I tap
The slate roof's peak, feel
The roots' far-sunk resonance.

In Sorrento, Maine

The whole house hangs from its peak
Forty feet on frayed light cord:
An exclamation point
Standing off dark wood burnish
Through sifting birch smoke. Mornings
I walk the upper porch, eye
To eye with birches. Today
I tilt my chair back into the wall.
The silence is an ambush
Just before it springs. Strands
Of hair brush my collar, pulse
Comes back through the chair.
                                        My wife
Says the foundation is crumbling,
And she may be right.
I'll grow a white pine from the cellar
Up through the roof to lean on,
And talk to my friend about animals
With fur—he's mad for black bears.
A cow moose with five-inch tracks
Wanders out of the deep shade
And stares hard:
                        Outside,
On our backs at the mossy southwest corner,
We watch the sun inch
Up spruce boughs and set
At their tips.

Fryeburg Fair

1 Oxen

Move yoke by docile yoke
fast as freezing water's flex
to burst its mold.
                    Blocks of lead—
the cleric dedication
they would split the earth
could they hitch the angle.

Spent, muzzles point like plummets.
Bodies mass in avalanche
at the needle's eye of the yoke's
bottleneck.
                    Big as eggplants,
eyes roll through hogsheads of skull
watching for ripples
at the bottom of the gorge.

2 Horses

No work like horses!
Masters of harnessed plunging.
Tidal furs whose throats are steam geysers.
Blood mains wander their bellies
out of the oases of shoulder pits.
The lost tribes of gunpowder
burl massive thighs and shoulders
into the load. Whose giddy eyes dance
like a double image of the sun
above the dune of their tongues.

Slick

for Marsha Henning

1

The outline of something huge
Underwater in the aerial photograph
(350 thousand gallons of fuel oil
Roll fallow, northeast of New Haven)
Close to where I rowed with a lobsterman at dawn
And chopped ice from his cabin door.
Choked to life, the engine's exhaust
Blobbed in my nose. Its iridescent glaze
Set my teeth at each other. His daughter:
I thought of her hard warmth and looked back
Where his house, two-story pendulum,
Struck through March dawn fog.

At noon, we lay in sheltered anchor
Off Great Wass Island's outer reach.
Sun brooded through overcast. The North Atlantic
Ground its gray heels beyond sight
Where the cloud bank squeezed through a slit
Between sky and ocean.
I picked a raw, crushed claw from the deck,
A tablespoon of jellied amino-water
Inside the low-domed limestone cave.
To listen, I thought, in the gull's beak
And the wind's lung, in the engine's cold death
For the solemn, sliding movement of earth
Over one edge of its life. Like mobiles,
Gulls balanced above the boat.
I hung on the rail, wanting never to go back.
At the end of sight,
Ridges blurred and wound into blue green
Ocean valleys. I felt my spine
Inch down, out of reach.
                    This oil

Could toast every toe on Beals Island
All winter: Woodwards, Beals, Alleys
Clustered in the cemeteries' nest
Of sad plastic flowers. Its shadow
Floats by the fishing shacks
Pitched along shore, like dark teeth
Pegged into a loose face.

2

We wound among buoys marking traps
We'd baited with stinking herring
And buried against sunrise.
We slid into dock, posed for a postcard.
The mainland bridge arced unsupported into fog
Like a smooth outer curl on large whelk shells.
Gulls stood the rails one-legged.
A speedboat
Skimmed like some incredible water spider
And glimmered through fog banks:
Leaps of thought along the channel
Past the smooth-shored cove
Where the road ends.
                              Where a line of sight
Falls back to the sea,
Someone built a miniature village
Around a guest book and sitting-room window
Without curtains. Across the street
I watched a man scrub potatoes
And lay them on a rock outcrop. Two Maine russets,
Each bigger than a large man's fists
Unblinking under dull foreheads, twin
Lobes of yeast
Raise Baptist and Jehovah's Witness churches
Into squat steeples, from bedrock and elemental muck.

Slick

I imagine signing the small-print pact, diving
To that life beside the sea.

I clasp someone's hand,
Another takes mine. We reel through shrouds
Of fog, our breaths wreath the air
Where we have been. The line grows
By numb toes: clam rakers,

Diggers of gristly sea worms, the lobstermen.
Women who tie their hair in scarfs
And sit all day in straight-backed wooden chairs,
Shucking the salt-quick life from raw clams.
We wind along the sea from nowhere, to the bridge

And the photograph. Oil
Ticks away from New Haven, off this page
And under the bridge. Darkening
The mirror of the sea,
Something begins to rise and plainly face us.

The Popping Tree Moon

No wind. Bare cold
Scampers on prickly squirrel claws. Numb
Edges of my feet grate the snowcrust.
Each hand palms its goose-fleshed thigh
The way fingertips read braille.
Falling is the worst thing
I can imagine.

The dog curls each paw, like fiddleheads
Caught in a May snap, leaves blood
And freezes at the sound:
                              crystal icebergs
Shatter: December's bones creak
Along their gnarl-grained age.
Something in the stark
Twilight-colored world
Gives way.
                    Sap and resin nests
Crack their yolks
Into a new year's darkness.

II

The Blue Dream

The American Porch

Spread-eagle deck of an ark.
Chained from a stern heaven stark against the sky,
Its wooden swing poses generations
Of black and white memory.
The stiff lap sways like a metronome
Through Sunday double-headers,
Moves on any breeze
As though someone has just left
To shuck corn for supper,
Or pitch sparks of dust between horseshoe stakes.
Or set out for work
On the sudden Monday morning
Of the twentieth century

Down the road that wound through bees
In elderberries.
Before the bend of those huge,
Silent afternoons, you could look back
Where percale curtains
Hung listless as carp out the kitchen window.
Frizzled at the gills, a patriarch blue spruce
Shook hands over the rail, as everyone dozed
And thought he dreamed.
                                    You
Never return. Chances are
Malaria got you, or a war bride.
The anchor half of the century
Flowers to atomic proportions. Imagine—
A pygmy reduced your skull to essential size
And sewed your lips shut.

Pig Heaven

One, so fat he'd have trouble
leaving the dugout
surrounds the two-fisted trophy-goblet
like a glass display case. A flimsy
aluminum foil mold
in the abyss of his mass, it reveals
his hands are his mother's
who brought him
to ease him out of himself.
                              His father
wants him home learning to weld. The boy
has never felt his body.
He dreams it is there,
seeing others dash through the flame
of a moment. Any moment
they choose. He is an angel
undefiled in Pig Heaven.
                              His soul
is like an opossum in adversity
first feigns death, then is buried
alive. He may live.
He may even wake up to see what
crawls out to survive.

Midwest Lemmings

1

Build below Ohio's flood mark
each year. the same foundation
a tornado ripped bare:
     "Sounded
like a big freight coming
the Chicago mail run but that's
after supper. my plate of ribs on the wall the floor
slapping my face.
     wash up each night stare
out the window
    where the funnel
shivered down the block"

2

Summer nights. moths
flood to death on back-porch bulbs.
parked outside the Dairy Freeze
boys tip pop tops
their faces green neon.
a girl lights up the phone booth
her lips glossy her long hair
tied up out of reach

Wisconsin Farm Auction

"Minneapolis, Midwest,"
McDonell says inside the airport.
"Okay. Show me the Great Plains."

Snowballs drop everywhere.
Sound drifts behind barns, back through
Wind-up victrolas in the yard and gathers
Under brass bed-frames picketing the lawn.
The auctioneer's assistant sidles to McDonell,
Stands where the mattress wants to be, plumps
An imaginary pillow. "Bet many a hired girl
Spent time here," palming
A brass post-head. Ruddy farmers stamp the snow.
Their denim jackets, lined in red and black squares
Flap over zippered sheepskin vests.
Surfer hair eggbeaten, McDonell
Raises his arms and puffs at the sky.

Twenty-five bucks for a buffalo sled-blanket!
Three pairs of stiff horse harness,
The collars like misshapen leather innertubes.
A wooden cash register. "McClaskey, Alliance, Ohio."
Enameled keys. Rings and works
Once the dust is brushed away. Potato drill:
He holds it sideways. "You got a crocodile,
Maybe alligator. Lookit his mouth. Clomp!"
He slides a cabbage grater's wooden box
Along its grooves. Snowflakes plop
On the steel blades. A bloodstained sheepskin coat
For a quarter. He looks like a Dalton brother,
Gunslinger in Acme boots.

We nail "collar horns" to the wall
(Two pairs are steamed ash,
One steel with metal ball-tips).
Bridle temples are brass rosettes and a string
Of ivory rings, dangling from an inch
To three and a half in diameter.
Dozens of buckles, cinches, huge
And little tongs, flutings and whorls
Heft like turtles, or bricks.
We buff the green with silver polish.
Solid bronze. Some pure brass! McDonell strings two
Around his neck.
"Indians gave away rivers for these."

The buffalo fur curls three dark brown inches,
Incredible coarse hoary stuff
So massive it looks artificial.
We throw it on the couch.
It defies the room, dwarfs everything,
Wants to rise up and thunder somewhere.
Lies dead weight around the shoulders when we wear it,
Pounding us breathless in minutes.
Perches rigid in a corner chair. We watch it sit
Higher than human.

That night McDonell was cold upstairs.
Somehow dragged the buffalo through the dark
To his bed,
And slept until noon.

Inside Cover, Anatomy Text, Mankato

1

Consider the Midwest belly
A fleshy billboard of blue veins
Big as the side of a barn
CHEW MAIL POUCH it says
Slouching in the weeds

2

Place a profile transparency of the belly
Over a Midwest map
Pittsburgh to Denver
Okie City to the border

3

Let us approach the belly
Fields remain, catch my shoes
following insect clouds that do things to the sun
plowed land falls downhill
                              all its life
                                    disappears
land's end under my heels
waves of topsoil:
                    firm, blood-black
the iridescent   moonlight sea

4

Plowshares turn Mankato's full belly
inside out. (it is a fight:
      knot the rein tips
      loop your neck
               under one armpit
      lean back on the knot between shoulder blades
      dig your heels against earth
                      plow
                            team.
never loop both arms:
          team spooks
          single trees snap
          you're up over the plow)

      listless with heat and boredom
arrowheads come
birdpoints: dull puff-eyed
obsidian ticks

5

You're a tooth
earth's a gum
the team's the dentist
with his pliers
of a plow

The Blue Dream

My problem is believing 10 thousand lakes.
Is there One Lady-of-the-Lakes
Or One for each? Do they choose Her
Brunette like the Chippewa,
Blonde for Scandinavia
Or five thousand apiece?
I can hardly imagine Minnesota.
Silent ladies
Floating on stark blue water.

I go see the governor and volunteer
For census taker of lake ladies.
He is deep in thought:
"Where is land for all these lake shores?
Four zeros," he mutters. "I am qualified,"
I swear. "Do statistics interest you?
Each resident might have a lake to himself
A day and night each year!" The governor
Stares at me. "Some Leech Lake Chippewa
Strides over Mississippi each morning:
One step across the true head, *Itasca*
Where it begins exhaling to New Orleans.
These are Minnesota facts!"

Great Molly Dick of states,
People are always overlooking you.
Say, what goes on and what gives
Up country there where no one lives?

2

Saturday night wrestling in Mankato.
Buffalo, Gully, Thief River Falls: places on a map.
Albert Lea, Bemidji veined in snow tunnels.
Deep bluish canyons of snow
Crisp as talcum blocks, insulate
And overwhelm. Snow turns back the senses
Until thaw, leaving us ourselves
To sour the clear air of St. Cloud, Long
And Blooming Prairie, Red Wing, Blue Earth
—Great geographic shoehorns!
Owatonna, Pipestone the sacred quarry, Bird Island,
Starbuck, Sleepy Eye.

I am wholly intimidated.
Minneapolis rises off the prairie like a cliff,
Wheat Growers' buildings are austere
Stolid-block keeps of American Gothic.
Its elevators are Knut Sodbuster's shins
In caricature.
But mostly space to draw a bead on.
Space
Like a hundred-mile-wide balloon full of helium
Bobs above White Earth and Red Lake,
Its boneless chest expanding limitlessly.
Its cord hangs like a torn strand of cobweb
From the ceiling that rises
Into Canada.

Crossing the Mississippi

Winesap's global fire stands in the river.
The sun rinses copper spires green.
Muskrat paddlewheels flush a pair of wood ducks,
Intricate, calm as Chinese brush drawings
In the last-lit, brilliant corner of dawn.

Blizzard!

"Wait it out at my place,
Two hundred yards back.
Not a serious walk." Denis Day, stockman,
Strolled offhand from Nebraska storm
To invite me.
                    Gas tank empty, snow
A windthrown wall of darts, sleeping bag
A raw pelt across my back, I never saw
The farmhouse until I'd lost my car.
                                    His pickup
Slid across the Platte, among clumps of Herefords
And their steaming calves: fur chips
Drifting through March. We wrapped one,
Fresh-licked, in burlap.
                        It froze, blown
Open-eyed in the truck's bed.
All day I saw the head
Toppling on its twisted neck, chestnut eyes
Staring back. How can wind
Shriek and echo through each cell? "Goes days,"
He said. "You miss her when she stops."
His rangy backbone of genes
Wound into door-frame corners.
Even his belly slouched. He said
Nothing more. Drank coffee, stared
At the windshield. Let me help
Carry the dead, and never
Asked my name.

Spontaneous California News

Spring has been sighted!
                against brown
          unblinking eyes of the coastal range

And finally appeared!
                in onshore fog
                      6 AM today
              ("feels like you're 26 again
                        back in California")

Terry sounds great!
                misses us
                    holds messages plump as figs

Spoke of living on the beach
Walking the cement boat's deck:
                      warm rain   sun
                      wandering sand

He saw it all! wonders most
                  when we're coming!

Doubtless I love him!
                Something fine's getting ready
                ("don't come any better")
                        and
I can't wait!

Six Days in July

Winnemucca, 13/71

Face down in a Sierra pool, my head steams. Numb all day until
this moment, I feel pine needles snap under my crouch and rasp
my fingertips. Counting their teeth: whorls on a rough thumb.
The bottom of the pool pulsates against my eyelids. Flying over
the Rockies between Denver and Grand Junction, I am swim-
ming through a microscope. Pinhead bugs crawl through valleys
of the Divide. A fleck of algae hovers in the mist—that's his leg!
the familiar leg of my friend. He'll take me to his hidden village
where we'll drink brandy together. I'll fall in love.

Chief Joseph Pass, 14/71

At Wells, cut right angle north. High desert, prairie, foothills: the sensation of surfacing with no more air in the tanks. I walked to a ridge blooming with sage, sat crushing leaves and rubbing the odor in my hair. Plucked a sprig to notch behind one ear. An old man has carried the mantle of dawn a long way and stoops to drape it around my shoulders. Above the road and power lines I enter the cleft of land and sky. The dog's fur in my hands is where I arrive.

Up Idaho's rock spine I caught the Salmon, flashing trout of a river throbbing past Hemingway's Sawtooths. *Life* called the photo as stiff-legged punter his favorite. The beer can hangs and hangs above his head. 600 miles on the nose away from yesterday. I breathe my best breath, crisp as a cedar chip.

Bowman Creek, 15/71

Anaconda. Slow coils glisten through every valley. Up the Bitterroots from Sula Station, log cabins are bins filling with bauxite, the last predator. West Glacier mountainsides are swept as though employees of aluminum-refining plants set invisible fires. At Moiese National Bison Range, shed and interlocked elk antlers rise thirty feet in the shape of a silo. The consternation a battery of guided antlers would cause, each of thousands of bone points darting for a different black heart! Seventeen miles below Canada, the ranger says follow standard precautions and the grizzly that ran over camp yesterday shouldn't bother. Sleep apart from your food supply in different clothes than you fry supper in. Be able to get up the nearest tree quickly. Squatting by the fire in a lodgepole stand of the Blackfeet mountains, I stare at the steel-tube bear trap, its door poised like a guillotine. Next tent, a woman who looks like the mother of all movie muleskinners turns her face along the firelight. Its bones stand out the way my knife sheath shows the blade's shape. She offers maul and wedges for me to split wood and crawls into her jeep for the night, taping the windows with newsprint.

Going to the Sun, 16/71

I stumble into the swelter of Browning, a housing tract rising like the mumps on the full life of the land. Holy mountains gleam in the west, their range jagged as shattered crystal. The road up Going to the Sun Mountain winds terrifyingly over mica-paved streams. At eye level with the wilderness an immense horizon of birch leaves waves like sunrise. I walk into the All-American Indian Days campground. There are two dancing rings, cottonwood limbs of leaves stacked around the edges for shade—the detail immediately ancient. A chanted throb drums beneath the gambling tarp, beaded sticks fly across centuries, odors of vinegar and deep-fat-fried potatoes. The sun drones all afternoon beside carney rides moving to Danny and the Juniors.

Devil's Lake, 17/71

Mountains sink away behind me. The Bear Paws hesitate at the southern horizon and shuffle along buffalo plains undulating in the final throes of reptile agony. I stop. Silence is the roar inside an ear: as it stalks prey a huge animal muffles the living sound of earth. Something is crushing and heating the air at twilight. A huge mouth whose throat stretches three states, opens. It is going to swallow towns like Havre whose fear of the plains is as transparent as its size. It is about to transform the fear of dying level into attention: listening for the next strong even heartbeat when all else has vanished. Earth-moving machines, grain elevators, bulldozers smash to their knees as the Thunderbird swoops up the sky from its thundercloud eyrie. The plains stop to watch it chase and pound the sky to earth with lightning blinks. A gas station franchiser is illuminated by horror as he stares down petroleum veins to the earth's center and the first fossil families' tentative gropes of feeling. The bird settles into Devil's Lake, its medicine nest. The slow, spasmodic dream of earth returns.

Bemidji: Holiday Ramblers, 18/71
for Marshal Phillips and Kurt Krueger

My seventh drive across country. I remember one day along Mormon roads in Utah: six hours without another car. The way sun struck brown and green slabs from the canyons. Today could be early November or late April: cold, wet, the wind unrolling highways anywhere through flat, bland Minnesota. In fear of the wind I stop at a cafe. I anticipate the waitress, her shy-smiling overweight desperation. I open the Fargo Sunday paper. White birch trunks glisten out of the gray morning like bones, making calm black moth patterns of drowning under ether. I remember wrapping picture frames in newsprint the fall I moved away to college. Suddenly, this is all the Midwest I knew fifteen years ago! The woods is a northern dialect I'm beginning to pick up again. I think of following the road through woods into distance and darkness, coming out . . . somewhere:

Stoplights and crossroads are clogged with caravans of travel trailers like tank or Conestoga columns. Pointing at maps like dozen-armed weather vanes, men wearing jackets branded with travel patches cluster around their leaders' hoods. Motor bikes and the turmoil of noisy picnics branch away from each trailer like spokes of a spider's web. This is their game. I see all the roads interlock at intervals to form a huge concrete net which is beginning to beach the country. Outside my motel, a stuffed moose stands with a mailbox welded around his neck and allows neither pets nor children.

III

Living like Indians

Living in the Tipi: When It Snows

During the night something is different.
Even before you open your eyes
you can tell—so very still.
A branch creaking or a tree rustling
sounds soft and far away.
From under the covers
you see shadows of lacing pins.
They look thick and fuzzy through the canvas.
Light is pale and diffused
as though it has come an exhausting way.
You peak beneath the door flap
and discover the whole world
folded into place.

Raccoon Dancer: Dream, Dance, Vision

1 Vision

I am Wanblee Ishnalla
On a rock shelf of skulls and hunger
I saw earth as a glittering crust of salt
Two huge and fierce hawks tear me away
They drop me and I fall a full day
I do not want to die
My blood spreads along the salt

                                    A raccoon licks me
Lightning stabs from his eyes
His breath is rancid and when I writhe
He bites me
Brother he says
Raccoon Dancer

2 Medicine

Moccasins trace the snake's path
A crow flutters on my back
Alive with mirrors my knife sheath
Led to earth by a Dog Soldier sash
A red pinch-bag of horsehair
The grass-stuffed raccoon

I come in peace
Red cheek patches
Raccoon's mouth and my blood
A spotted turkey dangles from my hair
For uncle's death
One notched eagle marches for first coup
I bring medicine to dance

3 Challenge

Shamazza drums and chants roar
Bells tremble and glisten in firelight
No one knows who wins the knife challenge

Who finds the snake's path
Who learns the secret of the drums

My knife searches air
My brother cannot find me
                        look where he comes

I feel the path   Yi!
My feet fly inside the drums
My knife parts the current of my brother's blood
He lies down bleeding
The river of his body floods
We drown inside the drum
Float down the high wind of the snake's path
To the center of earth

The spirit sips his blood
We scream that it might be ours

He leaps stronger than before
We dance together
Our legs break before morning
Yi!   A game of fire

My name is Wanblee Ishnalla
Raccoon Dancer

Coming Back

(Mt. Moosilauke, 29/x/72)

Six years without a climb. each step
shatters mud-water crystals: Sioux
keening in sunrise. rag-wrapped Bigfoot
froze grinning, right arm
still in peace: a petrified trillium.
I think of birdpoints heading wind,
ducks' backs quartering a storm.
smooth hairless black birch buds
crush into wintergreen. cool saltbeads
tingle on my back, and down.
finally I'm clear: rock meadows.
open ridge-scree
arching to summit like the instep of a spoon.

Two eagles hunt the ridge
against the smog belt overweighing Boston.

     kree kree kree:
          wet leather hinges muffled in moss.
fold wings
      shoot
         three hundred yards for my dog
but rise and loft away, seeing me
frozen in my tracks.
         their huge winging
painful as thumbnails' backbend: wings
barely hold something
together
      in the bodies' lifeknot.

Sun returns their rock-ribbed gloss
yards from my face

     their mirrored-sheen
         of underwing.

Pioneer Park

What it says

No Camping or Loitering by Picnic Tables
Closes 10 PM
No Dogs

What to do

Swim away. Start at the point where Menominees stood in 1807, P. mon Pier writes (in translation), watching woodland bison surge into the river "until the channel itself was full, yet rise again on the far bank like a sliding trail of horned rocks." Get to the other side. Take a while. Take fifty thousand years, so that when you stand and look back there will be a sky of neon bowling alleys and funeral homes' brick facades. Woodland and plains buffalo will return the next morning. They will have stumbled into the hollow your absence caused and slid, as down a tunnel, back to us. They will mill out of your ears and churn about on the river's bank, watching the other shore with a light in their eyes one sees when looking at bonfires some distance through fog.

Why

To stand among large, heavy animals. To ride them, the hollows of their backs falling away like mountain meadows so that you remember your childhood of walking on moss in spring and studying for hours ant-sized yellow and blue blossoms. Noticing how closely a ripe sunflower's head resembles an insect's compound eye. To become a constellation:
Boy on Fur Triangle.

Will the Real National Bird Please Disappear

1

Invited up to the big house for holiday potluck,
His tail fan spreads
Into glossy, wind-lurched indignation.
Wings taut as a dried bat's
Solemnly drag the dust, scoring the boundaries
Of no-man's-land. Strutting,
His scaled shins tick like pendulums.

2

This feathered mushroom blooms,
As ripples on a pond wander into weeds
At the forgetful water's edge.
Following the carcass from capture
To skeleton, we recognize ourselves
In the mirror of the wishbone, squinting
From the junta of the breast!

3

This is true nationalism!
Eating what we love without confusion.
Crazed by blood, turkeys peck through each other's wounds,
To death, in minutes. We scatter leaves
To bare this gathering terror
That locked the savage,
Murderous and innocent
In his tracks.

The Fall Meal

More relatives leave each day,
kick their chairs back from steaming full plates
sensing something prime: as though each leaf
falls with a smaller clue
to the rare point of their lives, and each
walks out a different door he doesn't shut.
The house is all doors on frames—
xylophone of careens, seizure
of slams: heard heart attacks!
Alone in the wind finally, trout
swim across the table of zinnias, a moose
grazes in the sink—day and the wind
bear us like a benevolent net.
It is joyous, and through the flickering doors
we catch glimpses everywhere.

The Last Indian

for Allen Ouellette

He juggles the quiet terror of the wilderness
For what is unusual.
Tenuous
As echo, disturbing the creek bed
Less than twilight,
Conscious only of his feet
Sliding before his shadow, he passes downstream to the reach
Of the last branch.
                Where he began
Brooks tumble like cirrus,
Grass and sandstone-colored trout
Scale the attitudes of current.
Their arrow-flashings flush my ears with blood,
Their sunburst, lightning rises
String my eyes on rawhide.
                Once
His shale, potholed eyes
Stare from my creel in murderous pride,
He tries to gurgle his ears clear, to breathe.

Living like Indians

for Sam and Suzy Cohen

The horizon shimmers.
Shaggy horns and the crossed bones of death
Mark concrete pods of nerve gas:
Vaults of poison that cannot be buried
Long enough to die! Our one-life stops
Poise, like pitchforks
For anything that lives. We are mad
In love with the dead ends of dust.

Comanches
Rode as though they grew from horses' shoulders,
And believed death was a gift
Blooming with the bitter warmth of morning stars in winter
To fulfill their whorled lives.

                        To move as smoke drifts . . .

One dream of America
A petrified foetus crouched in Plymouth Rock.
Only earth survives
Shamen said, and the sea
Tumbles from a shell held to the ear.

IV

Realizing What Has Passed Is Gone

Realizing What Has Passed Is Gone

1

No one understands the film.
Still, silent moments, how
The bullets strike.
Frantic, we yank a slide and blow it up—
Fail-safe memory of one day
We rode to Dallas in a black, open car.

The wall clock's arms point and funnel,
Grinding the fine powder of the stars
Closer to quicksilver.
Faces in the crowd contort, trying to realize
What the bullets are coming to.
Theirs are a fighter's nerves
As his glass jaw begins to crack.
Feather-delicate lobes, pink as lungs
Through the brow's clear resin
Take in the lobo slug
And bloom, atomically.

2

Before a portable black-and-white
With drifting vertical hold,
We crack a pop top
And watch the pole-vaulter in the ad
Rise like a missile,

Hover far beyond us. Up,
Out in the humming ice of space
The bullet approaches lunar docking
And the piston-vaulter falls like a shot.

A hollow-nosed tidal wave
Slams into the Sea of Tranquility.
Boot prints petrify on this
Eternal stare.

3

In the end, our heads ache
From just one beer that fall afternoon
Clear as a bright bulb.
When the lights come on again
Years later, our slide
Brushes the projector bulb, and mushrooms
Out of the picture.

Nothing eases the dynamic
Building up thinner than air.
Nobody knows anymore, what
Our travels have found.

On the Way to the Burying Ground

Out in the open
I trip on a laceless shoe, pressed thin
As one scrapbook carnation.
Snow and rust-flecked septic tanks
Perch beside a shallow ditch. The frostbitten Ohio
Shoulders through its valley. At this edge
Everything trails off.
Bare trees lean out of winter. Telephone poles
Suture the incredibly refined wounds
Of this small town. Powder snow
Hides the tracks,
And a cold freight cracks along dawn
Cutting me off, looms through beeches
As though it is a great weasel leaping the river
Back to his country.

One Dream of Cleveland

Evening settles like gravel-road dust
And begins disappearing in me. Its grains rise
With the crowns of my goose bumps.

A small mongrel begs,
Perches & hammers, finally sticks
In the business end of a St. Bernard.

Behind a screen door an undershirt bellows.
Saw-toothed with rage,
The voice collects with a burst
And blows off a shotgun.

The mongrel staggers and rips through
The magnetism of his flesh,
Blurs to indifference: hollow-nosed slugs
Fired into sand. His intestines whirl
Like great bloody wreaths.

St. Bernard crawls back, the mongrel still
Strung wriggling inside.
The dogs streak along their blood
And struggle to stand. To rise! Then
Splay on asphalt,
Face each other
And die.

On the Occasion of the Cuyahoga River's Burning

Wound lush from its mouth

The Eries called it *crooked*, farmed here
                    fished, gentle and fat
                    lake perch, whitefish
                    dunes of freshwater shells

Rubbed out by Senecas   1611
                    imagine
    before sturgeon (broke the surface like logs)
            passenger pigeon
            woodland bison
                    wickiups
        smolder down sandy drainage:
                    cherry orchards
                    truck farms, huge nurseries

Moses Cleveland
                    Germans   Czechs   Slovaks   Poles
                    chain the wilderness, build homes
                    foundries, mills, he said.
                    We run with the nation. send the rest
            to the sky, the land
            bears our promise, the river

Burns at its mouth: a trencher of oil
                    the elements sustain attack from

Fire in the pyre!
                    in the last fifty years
                    the lake aged 15 thousand
                                sheet of flame
                    flows like a broken mirror:

    Fifteen thousand years' bad luck

Hurricane!

Struck in the morning, veered west
of Mobile to escape. Natchez
by nightfall, the storm's eye
zeroed on us. Hugged the full jail's
lee brick wall, swelled all night
in the full blood of the wind.
Delivered at dawn.
The eye-rolling, fishbelly sky
roared like an ear struck numb.
Against all advice, we drove
to Baton Rouge, bobbing through
hollows of rowboats. The brakes
drifted. Frayed and sizzling
missed connections, the whole day
we never saw the sun.

Green River Rendezvous

Patching my flat in his Esso
Luis Rey talks. I study some Arapahoe
Crouched in the corners of his eyes.
"There's a kind of fort, and a play
About the fur trade. You swear
You was back in the old days."

Old Luis Brushhead, don't you know
You run the one kind of fort.
Still, one and a half centuries, this
The last camp before rendezvous
And the first night coming back,
You could be right. Sick,
Scared, the Eldorados and Cougars
Pitch a makeshift camp
At the premium pump. The fires
Get away with everything but ashes
During the first watch.
The mosquito netting leaks. All night
Beaver slap the dammed waters
Of the middle ear,
Laughing through their pelts.

Truck Stop

Pushed all night from Utah to tell you boys—
chain up before them mountains. I didn't
and I'm lucky to be here talking.
Hotcakes & Log Cabin, honey, links & twin
sunny-sides, hey. And just tell java
to walk out here once.

I recall an early run. My brakes give out
on one of them Wyoming border passes.
Slid into Cheyenne, both hands on the wheel
and two rows of teeth.

Ed says he won't eat, hell.
Gonna stay in the crapper.
Smell's better, such as it is,
account of the black nigger down the counter
and his white gal, who don't look
old enough to. Maybe
we oughta take Ed's plate in. Naw,
send Amos.

Crossroads

Three tourist cabins fall to dry rot
behind a panhandle cafe. A screen door
plops on its face, like a bass
falls back in a pool of sunset, as though a man
stuns his boot on the doorsill, trying to catch his
heart before it bursts.

A tabby tiptoed through fresh snow. I saw
a shotgun riddle her into a furry sieve of blood.
Poppies bloomed from her ears.
Pronghorn antelope plunge into the cafe's walls
clear to their Adam's apples.
They see the failure of their horn's wishbone tines
to reach an even branch, their glass
paperweights of eyes amazed
as though they turn astonished cretins.

The cross hairs gauntlet of highways
pierces four horizons.
The wind imagines tree leaves,
spending the day soothing their edges.
Small dust tornados march in random columns.
Farm ponds look like consommé, their water red
far down like paper slashes.

The Film *California and Back*

1

Pour a cool riesling
Through the credits. Pan midnight
Orchids: bare black girls
Sunning in driftwood, their thighs' burnish
The uneven luster of tide-smooth eyes
In black abalone shells.
Documentary beach walk: one couple
Sandwiched in blankets. A wedding
In the sand. Hard-rock crests with the surf
Just out of reach. The bride's family
Plows up in a Cadillac limousine. Eucalyptus
Hovers at the edge of the palate
Pungent as an amputee's memory of touch.

2

The Midwest April of lilacs
And honey-bellied bees: Sunday morning
At the Arbutus Cafe. Sleepy
River town square, white
With a taut, pristine
Judgment-day fear
That claws the eyes like sun glare
And will not filter.
Let the camera in behind us.
Assume staring, murmurs, brown
Linoleum and formica. The urinals
Look smelly. Home fries and biscuits
With each order. Toe held to the wall,
A radio chirps Lawrence Welk hymns.
Man faces wife in a booth and belches
At champagne bubbles. While he pays up
She throws a mother's look and clomps out
Embarrassed to sway the wooden floor.

3

Blanket sandwiches, Cadillac schooners,
Strawberry trees. Egg yellows
On toast crust, eucalyptus
Beneath our fingernails. Our breaths
Pass out in humid traces
And are sucked back: the ponderous, terrified
Headlong rush of a calf that's lost her way
And is catching up.

V

Fear of Home

*for Bruce Curley and Firebird Flynn
in the mountain stronghold*

Stopping in Donner Pass

My feet left earth last
A Conestoga month east
(Shimmering snow-dawn in the Wasatch).
I step out and end
A six-hundred-mile stride—
                    The far, frosted fists
        Of Wasatch. Salt Lake City.
        Swimming in salt lakes, unmarked
        Bobbing graves, the low veil of tears
        At sight's end.
        I felt my car drift in the desert.
        The mirage of control
        Climbs a terrible gray slope
        Too late. Donner in despair
        Wanders half a mile below.
        Twelve-foot snow cliffs throw him back—

Into California.
        So much of him here, crouched
        In manzanita bushes
        Spitting mouthfuls of blood. Hiding out
        Hoping for spring.

He almost made it.
Ten miles: Grass Valley, bees,
The bubbling Yuba.

Waking Up

The clock, for instance
Taps each second through the wall
Fifty feet away. The hummingbird
Hangs from a pastel knot of blossom
And transcribes
Like a furious light bulb. A black
Cigar-butt-sized lizard
Freezes on a charred kindling twig
Inches from my nose, and stares at me,
An incredible weariness
About his quick body, as though he knows
The sun has shrunk him from a dinosaur.
Eyelids flick like camera
   Shutters. The mechanisms stick
On an oily, water-vapor glaze. Backstage,
Scenery shifts: eras of sound
Slip into echo, the eyes clear
As their memory. Fast as a fly
He steps to my arm—
I've forgotten and eased it
Like a root, into the dust. Slipped
Staccato within moments, he
Has me in his strange
Rhythm. Each claw
Tightens my skin into so many
Drumheads. His shadow
Cold as a burn, his cool body
Pulses in the sun. I've never seen
This patch of skin! I stare at the first step
Along a new trail
And wonder where it's ever been. We
Share it all, standing alone.

Getting Crazy in the Garden

1

The lemons bloom by knife
Into six-petaled lilies. Tequila,
Acrid distillate of century plants.
A mound of salt. The hundred-year fruit
Of lemon flowers bears within us,
While the sun shinnies up redwoods
And prepares to take the sea.
Plants held all day in heat
Shimmer to rest at the edge of earth
And sway to drink.
My dog sleeps in the sun. I squint
Through the chill, unwavering eyeball
Of sky, and scratch after a slow breeze
Walking the slats of her rib cage.

2 (twilight)

Tomatoes:
Pungent pincushions. Silk-thatched peaks
Of sweet corn. Zucchini and cucumber logs
Jam rows of turgid earth. Knothead
Broccoli and cauliflower, cousins,
Stand on tiptoe, staring in
Each other's keyhole. Melons loaf
In a Persian daydream's sweet conclusion.
Eggplant and green pepper swell exotic hides
As kidney and heart.

3 (morning)

Musky love-apple plants
Preen dewy feathers of vine. Clear gray eyes
Inch along cauliflower leaves. Eggplants
Rise like Mayan temples, blood-
Purple leaves beating the sky.
Bees like fuzzy dirigibles
Bob among huckleberry blossoms.
I feel the far edge of silence
And understand stereophonic sound: suddenly
A Mason jar's trademark,
Distorted under a quart of water, goes
When the glass empties,
And remains. My perspiration gathers,
Slips to the end of hair strands
And drops: sweatblossoms
Sown back to earth.

Watching Animals

Scuba divers raid abalone reefs
Of sea otters' only food.
Slow, blinking primevals,
They surface and sun
Glints away from their masks.
Slowly starving, the otters
Bob like fur-covered bottles
And clap,
Raucous with delight
As children at recess.

Climbing a Redwood

The problem is where to take hold
No limbs for eighty feet
Thick flaky sheets of bark
Woodpeckers get lost behind

"Stand under one
Press into the trunk and look up
Feels good to do that"

Last of the old gods
Twenty centuries of thin dust
Rising almost out of sight
Toward some promise the insects make out
And drone back each afternoon

Cambium changes into new layers
We swim all the way up
The sweet dark spring each tree caps
Ears popping blood jumping eyes
Search beyond the crown
                    Where we've burst
A billion insects hum away and the tree
Inches into the vacuum

At last we sway to the wide mysteries
West on the stark endless sea

Lotusbound

for John Jourdane, friend and stranger

Picnic

We drive through two, sleepy
Sheet metal roof towns
Peter Lorre could wander out of.
The rest is Anaheim, the same smog
Blunders over pineapple fields.
We picnic below Kaena Point
Where the road gives out and the winter surf
Marches in thirty-foot crests.
Where drunk, barefoot Navy guys
Bomb tidal-wave warning sirens
With Gallo jugs of Pacific Ocean.

It all seems to gather on this tight
Little island: construction machines'
Unearthly shrieks and wrenchings,
Huge scars on a small creature
Caught unaware,
Slowly being beaten to death.

Japanese TV

Sumo wrestlers sow pinches of salt
On the screen. Their feet
Seem to rise from taproots,
Their immense, stylized bodies
Collide with medieval impact
Among Peter's bansai pines
And miniature porcelain.
We sip warm sake. Suddenly their crouch
Is Trout's, learning to walk!
He breathes lightly as a finch in his crib.
I try to plow the dark loam
Between child and Sumo crouch,
Before giving it to Peter who will thrive there.
But I am borne in a thimble of sake
Snoring like a dog.

The Bishop Museum

Iwi and o'o, birds plucked
For Kamehameha's
Woven feather robes: royal shrouds
For the ends of their species.
The yellow and red plumage
Made him appear to be wrapped in gold.

Felled in mountains,
Dragged by hand to the beach.
Outriggers fashioned from huge koa trunks.
Thousands launched
And the trees are gone.

A knife handle's inlay, precise
As braided rawhide
Or porcupine quill embroidery. Strange
As slow turtles' shells, diced
For the mosaic palm-bed.

A large bone fishhook,
The eye so marvelously round
I think it the bone's structure
And stare long minutes,
Trying to imagine sinewy body ropes.
Polished on centuries of sharkskin,
The long shank
Bears mother-of-pearl as lure. For barb:
A glossy shark's tooth!

Wired from the ceiling,
Seventy feet (a Greyhound bus) of blue whale
Flukes for the hook, its opposite side
Stripped to the bone
Beside Tahitian gowns and cymbals.

Nightscape

Waikiki hotel bars
Are livid with servicemen.
We walk the beach where the Royal Hawaiian's
Grass-shirt floor show glitters at the sea.
Polynesian Jim Crow, John says.
A mainland couple in evening clothes
Examines their Mercedes' fender, fingers
Almost touching the damage. A drunk
Handcuffed Hawaiian moans: Hate Haole!
Kill him all!
                    We sit over the water,
A wooden taffrail for balcony
And drink rum limes, the whole place
Quiet and deserted. This, one last
Good bar. City lights swarm
Like an horizon-wide beacon.
I've surfed this beach, John points
In the dark. When I leave
I'll sail out at night, alone.
The sun will come up
And only sea around me.

Lotusbound

"Landed in Papeete, one of few
South Pacific jet strips.
After six days on a Matson liner
Of bored, rich, empty old people, a fleck
Became jagged peaks of island, blue green
Against hovering quilts of mist. A lighter
Came out through the reef and I got off
For a month. Without communications,
A radio receiver for weather, I became
Less bone and skin than essence
Between the sound of the waves hitting the reef
And the singing and dancing:
Two constant roars.
Drummers changed and singers slept
But it never stopped, as though closing
The sea out, or keeping touch
And rhythm with water meeting sand.

"Four years in Oahu, I'm still unstrung.
These young Oriental girls,
Little lotus blossoms of desire—
Micronesian, Rarotongan, Malaysian princesses
By the trace of languor in their blood
And the twitch of wrens about their hands.
They'll marry somebody's brother,
A Swede from Keokuk unmarked by thought,
His smooth oak forehead
Wallowing in low-level abstraction.
I forget my shoes in bars. I write
One poem a year. I've got to get off
This fucking island!"

Hiking

We study blood drops scattered in orchid bowls,
Banyans' aerial-root forests,
An overwhelming harmony of odors.
Mangrove roots wrestle every step on the two-mile hike
To Manoa Falls. A crab spider
Baits one water-sparkling filament
From the ceiling-surface
Of foliage, his tint and textures
Those of a bright, enameled broach.
Trout cries out, cocks his head
And reaches.
The peculiar bronze mud
Stains our pores and scrubs out hard.
I think of ichor,
Rarified blood of the gods.
Wound with vines, young trees
Look like the flayed lengths
Of a human leg.
Bamboo clusters spray
With photographic unity: Chinese
Brush drawings, quiet bursts
At tropic random.

Surfing

A quarter mile off Waikiki,
My seven-feet-four pigboard
Floats solid as a waterlogged piano.
John brought me every stroke:
Waxing the board,
Belly-flopping, angling through white water
Or leaning back, both hands on the board
For the slap of head-on waves.
Get inside, he said, where they foam.
Lie down and feel the power. Sometime
You'll just want to stand. Everyone
Does that on his own. I slide away,
As intimidated here as on shore.
I barely walk the same beach
As Hawaiians, whose bodies' burnish
And long hair, glossy as a crow's back
Seem to grow from the white sand.
Island boys and girls slide past
On phosphorescent
Fiberglass meteor trails.
Behind me, the roar says I'm out too far.
I turn into a blind-alley collision.
Bigger waves rise at sea. I have one
Terror of water: the falling back.
I paddle frantically. Water stings my hand!
Nettle barbs, tentacles of short circuit
Hollow my fingertips. I stare down
In the great salt darkness
And fight the sensation to roll.
Goose flesh splashes my shoulders
Until my knees slide their jellied joints
And lock.
            I'm standing!

Lotusbound

In the pit of a wave, throwing me
Against stark, furrowed Diamond Head
Like a science fiction movie
Lurching toward Mars' surface. In that fine gaze,
I sweep on a moment's hinge
Above the sea.

Kamehameha Ridge Trail

The hugh conch held to his lips
Like a piccolo, John hones
A deep resonance.
"Shells speak what the body holds.
Now the mountains know it's us."
A spider crawls out of the conch
And he brushes it off. "Black widows
Like living here." The sign reads *Kapu.*
"Very strong 'Keep Out,' " he smiles.
"My private trail."

Crushing lemon eucalyptus leaves
For their fresh, dry smell,
We duck trail-wide cobwebs
And stop when the sun reveals
Great mandalas
Woven at the forest edge.
Rising steeply, we try
Not to step on any growing thing
And break through trees in two hours.
Valley, sky, Kamehameha Ridge Trail
Ahead. Resilient New Zealand ironwoods,
Their lacy needles "drawn like blown cloud"
Basho "couldn't stop dreaming of roaming."
Fifteen hundred feet below,
Oahu Country Club fairways
Stretch up Nuuonu Valley. Punchbowl
Cemetery further: a dead volcano's base
Full of grass. Honolulu.
The broad crescent sweep of Pacific.

We hunker on Lookout Rock like baboons,
Staring in the rain which shrinks our clothes

To skin but for pocket lumps.
"Always lichen first," John points
Down the boulder's side.
"Moss, then grasses and trees
Crack rocks like ice cubes.
Fifty thousand years, we'll be sitting
On an anthill."
I look down, following
A sickle-shaped koa tree's leaf
Across Nuuonu Valley
Far as I can see. Green and brown
Ti spots, ferns, ohia and sandlewood
Pulse like the side of a living thing.
"I get high up here," John says,
"Just looking. It's like diving:
I hang in the water, feel like never coming up.

"I decide not to die. Once,
John Muir climbed a big pine
To watch a snowstorm.
He'd have liked this rain!" John Muir,
I think, the right sequence of rock holds
Coming to him on Mt. Ritter
After total confusion.
                              Far off,
From the molars of the Koolau Mountains
Rain sheets unfurl
Across the whole sky.
At once I recall this rain's sweep
In the shimmer of northern lights
And, soaked to the skin,
I shiver.

Last Day: To the Airport

Alicia, Peter's girl
Passes a paper sack of watermelon seeds,
Chinese delicacies she dried and seasoned
In ginger and anise, her favorites.
She's never been to the mainland.
"What of Nebraska," she asks,
Nesting faintly damp jasmine leis—
Soft mouths of blossoms—around our necks.
"Peter won't tell me." The breeze
Of her voice flutters around us.
                                        He stops
Outside a rickety cemetery
On a splendid valley's slope
Rising like a funnel wall, and says
"Last century this was a mass grave
For Chinese laborers. At night it's still filled
With ghosts, visions, weird
Flute and drum music. Hawaiian burial caves
High up on the eastern rim
Charge Manoa Valley with spirit vibrations.
One afternoon of misty rain
While I was taking pictures, a particularly brilliant
Full double-rainbow
Appeared over the cemetery.
The wooden gate, mountains, a windswept palm
And the rainbows—all balanced in the view finder.
But the camera froze in mid-click,
Broke forever."
                        He stops
In his peculiar way,
Seeming to hang with great effort, seeming
Unable to say everything.
I understand, Peter.

Lotusbound

This time I have jumped with you
Into the fusion
Of what appears, and what we feel
We see, I want to say, but cannot.
I can not. Trout cries in my lap
And slaps the window at a fly. Silk
Curtains of rain quiver over the car.
A large rainbow sags like a branch heavy with fruit,
And we're late.

Fear of Home

for Peter Nelson

Windfall woods. A leaning pine
Stretched into fur, reared and stared
And slowly blinked. I stood, pissing,
Eye to eye with a black bear. My heart
Jackhammered into my knees. We backed away
As slowly as growth, the way limbs
Slip into twilight. Shadows
Filled our space.

I have died to be living here
Where trees grow for keeps,
Gaunt and passionate as statues, and finally
Split up, into dreams.
These sweet canyons are the heaven of bears.
The sky opens like the century to them.
I am covering ground thinking of home.

And wondering where. Moss grows lopsided
Over there. Trails vanish
Into the swamp like rows of stitching
On a prickly scalp. Fireflies
Or foxfire sputters downhill
Toward the last hollow tree.

Pitt Poetry Series

COLOPHON

The poems in this book are set in the Monotype version of Times Roman, a typeface originally designed for the London *Times*. As the virtues of the type became apparent, its popularity increased until it has become a modern classic. The book was printed directly from the type on Warren's Olde Style paper by Heritage Printers, Inc. It was designed by Gary Gore.